What's Another Word for Thesaurus?

Peter D. Carlisi

WHAT'S ANOTHER WORD FOR THESAURUS?
First Edition

Published by:
Biographical Publishing Company
95 Sycamore Drive
Prospect, CT 06712-1493

Phone: 203-758-3661
Fax: 253-793-2618
e-mail: biopub@aol.com

Copyright © 2014 Peter D. Carlisi
First Printing 2019

PRINTED IN THE UNITED STATES OF AMERICA

Publisher's Cataloging-in-Publication Data
Carlisi, Peter D.
What's Another Word for Thesaurus?/ by Peter D. Carlisi.
1st ed.
p. cm.
ISBN 1733812024 (alk. Paper)
13-Digit ISBN 9781733812023
1. Title. 2. Humor. 3. Puns. 4. Wordplay.
Dewey Decimal Classification: 817 American Wit and Humor
BISAC Subject:
    HUM018000 HUMOR / Form / Puns & Wordplay
Library of Congress Control Number: 2019916721

Roses are red,
Violets are blue.
Please buy my book,
So that I can retire too!

DEDICATION

I am dedicating this book to my wife, Chris, of 32 years for her continued love and support. Her tireless efforts have had a direct impact on the success of our two children, Peter and Richard, especially during my lengthy absences which were necessary in the performance of my sales career. I had the peace of mind knowing that our house was always a home and that she was always there for us.

THE CHAPTERS

CHAPTER 1

A RATHER UNUSUAL QUESTION

Is harness racing the Amish version
of NASCAR?

Do you think that they ever recalled
thermometers due to traces of
tuna in the mercury?

Is a small catamaran referred to as a
kittenmaran?

If one fails to pay his exorcist,
will they be repossessed?

If the Sunday morning television
religious shows are on cable TV,
would this be referred to as
Pay Per Pew?

If the <u>President</u> is elected by
the Electoral College,
shouldn't the <u>Vice-President</u> be elected by
the Electoral High School?

How do we clear the backlogs
in our courts?

JURIS PRUNEJUICE

Isn't the term *Civil War*
actually a contradiction of
two words?

Why are there wanted posters?
Wouldn't it have been easier to
arrest the people when they
took their pictures?

What good is a photographic memory
if you are out of film?

If one goes to bartender's school,
do they need to pass the Bar Exam?

If your computer is infected with a virus, it never develops an immunity.

Shouldn't this be called a computer bacteria?

If you are going to breed dogs,
should they be required to
attend a pre-canine course?

Does one get a pound cake
for their dog's birthday?

In those parts of the world where there is
6 months day and 6 months night,
do parents tell their kids to be
home by April?

Is it OK to run on a
"Don't Walk" signal?

Is writing a book
an infringement on a
dictionary's copyright?

Is getting a "C" in Spanish the same
as getting a "Yes" in English?

Do people in the South,
who might own sled dogs,
get their animals to run
by saying "GRITS"?

Is it safe to drink water in a
genuine Mexican restaurant?

Do electric candles in churches mean
that there are no special intentions
during peak demand hours?

Is the Tower of Pisa actually
an ancient sun dial
that is adjusted
for daylight savings?

Can skunks smell one another?

Was tap dancing invented by
a serious cockroach issue?

Did the horse whisperer ever ask the horse:

"Hey, why the long face?"

CHAPTER 2

DID YOU EVER NOTICE:

Did You Ever Notice:

Store clerks will check for counterfeit bills,
BUT customers rarely, if ever,
check their change?

When all the stores start to display
their Christmas decorations,
that Halloween is just around the corner?

Did You Ever Notice:

That one can never seem to cut a
grapefruit into equal halves?

The best pizza will come in a plain
white box with no name on it?

Did You Ever Notice:

That the shape of the State of New Jersey
looks like a left profile of
General Charles de Gaulle?

That a large cheese pizza and a
regular man's haircut usually cost
pretty close to the same amount?

Did You Ever Notice:

On a 7-day weather forecast,
the actual weather on the 7th day
is rarely the weather that had been forecast?

That some old cemeteries
look like giant chess boards?

Did You Ever Notice:

The subject of *spelling* in school
is the only subject that receiving the
correct answers ahead of time
is not cheating.
NO EXCUSES for poor grades.

Your alarm clock can only go
OFF if it's ON,
but cannot go
ON if it's OFF.

Did You Ever Notice:

That the *Entertainment Book* never
has a discount coupon for
next year's *Entertainment Book*!

CHAPTER 3

MY OWN OBSERVATIONS

THE UPSIDE OF THE NEUTRON BOMB:

At least renters are eligible
to get back their security deposit.

That 10 pound hairy mut running around
your neighborhood may actually be
a police dog working narcotics.

The furthest one can travel
is only halfway around the world
because after that point,
they are on the way back!

After all the discussion and debate on
climate change, and to put it simply,
the reason we have climate change
is because climate changes.

Before I got married,
all of my kitchen spices
could be found in the salt shaker.

Our happy marriage traces back
to our first date when we went skiing –
and it's been downhill ever since.

The strangest thing happened the other day:

While weighing myself
on a coin operated scale –
I lost 75 pounds
and my lucky number
turned out to be my former weight!

The upside of having low self esteem
is the opportunity to find money on the street
as you are always walking around
with your head down.

HELPFUL HINTS:

After buying a book
and putting your name in it for identification,
for added security,
circle the page number
that corresponds to your house number.

When sending your young child to school
with money for a book fair, etc.,
consider doing this:

Write the serial number of any
paper currency that he/she may be carrying.
This should clear up any issue that could arise
concerning whose money it is.

Wouldn't it be easier if airlines
did their passenger loading
by having passengers with window seats
enter first?

To parents with toddlers
who are buying a new car:

Select an interior color that matches
your children's favorite juice flavor.

FAT FREE FOOD:

Does this mean that the food contains no fat?

OR

Does this mean that the fat
contained in the food is free?

HELPFUL HINTS:

When parking at a concert or similar event,
park close to the street rather than
the entrance to the event.
The 2 minute walk is better than
the 20 minute traffic jam in the parking lot
after the event.

To keep track of batteries in a smoke detector,
put a date label on the batteries.
Also, put a date on the device itself
to insure proper replacement times.

You are not old until people
huddle around your birthday cake
to stay warm.

The toughest part of working from home
is that when I call in sick,
I keep getting a busy signal.

If you are purchasing a fly swatter –
buy at least 2.
(In case a fly should happen
to land on the first one).

In a murder-suicide situation,
sequence is key!

REMEMBER WHEN:

Going online meant that the
bathroom was occupied.

A broken clock is always
correct twice a day.

A suggestion on how to keep down
the cost of space exploration:

If planning a voyage to Mars,
plan the trip at least 21 days in advance
and have the astronauts spend
one Saturday night on the Martian planet.

If one throws unused ice cubes on the lawn,
they are merely watering
with time release capsules.

Any acid that can burn through anything
cannot be containerized.

To all college students:

Strive to get a 4.0,
but definitely not on a breathalyser.

ON GAMBLING:

I stopped following the horses
because the horses that I followed
always seem to follow other horses.

The ultimate example of good luck:

When you get a gravy stain on
your new golf shirt and the stain
is shaped like an alligator.

Could the famous "Goose Step" marching
actually be a result of
soldiers marching behind horses?

The possums in my neighborhood
are actually pretty smart.
I saw one the other day who had
the presence of mind to place
tire tracks over it's body.

CHAPTER 4

MY DEFINITIONS

To all you folks
that take an **XL** in clothing size –
cheer up, you are actually
a size 40 in Roman numerals.

Isn't "behind your back"
really by your stomach?

Just to set things straight:

The **International Date Line** is <u>NOT</u>,
I repeat, <u>NOT</u> a 1-900 number.

A **Cold War** is an argument between
you and the landlord for adequate heat.

MY DEFINITION OF DIETING:

No slices of pizza
while waiting for a pie to go.

POLYUNSATURATED:

A dehydrated parrot.

GERMAN MEASLES:

When one breaks out in tiny swastikas.

CAMEL:

A horse designed by committee.

SOUL MATE:

Someone you would eat fish with.

MERMAID:

A deep sea Diva.

What is the correct term for a boomerang that does not return to the person who launches it?

Answer: "A Stick."

Legal Terminology:

ATTRACTIVE NUISANCE:

A cockroach with a really great body.

INDENTURED SERVANT:

A butler with false teeth.

STATISTICAL FACT:

If your parents didn't have any children,
chances are that you won't either.

Medical Terminology:

SINUS RHYTHM:

Could this mean that one has
mucus coming out of both nostrils
in equal amounts?

INCARCERATED BOWEL:

When one gets his butt thrown in jail.

TONGS:

Instrument to pick up food
while people are watching.

CHAPTER 5

HOW'S THAT AGAIN?

Somebody walked off
with my pedometer.

Go by my picture,
my looks don't do me justice.

Concerning drinking and driving
on Independence Day:

"He who goes forth
on the 4th, with a fifth,
May not go forth on the 5th."

If <u>fish</u> is thought to be a brain food,
then consider the word *seafood*
spelled backwards.

Concerning unemployment:

The pay is lousy
but the hours are great!

I wonder if they will ever make a movie
out of a self help book
on conquering TV addiction,

Don't forget to recycle your notice
for that upcoming paper drive.

Does one snack before dinner
because they can't eat on an empty stomach?

Is *insomnia* worth losing sleep over?

If EMTs take law courses,
maybe someday they can
chase their own ambulances.

The early bird catches the worm,
but the second mouse gets the cheese.

Never put off until tomorrow
that which can be put off
until the day after tomorrow.

My neighbor thinks that
he may be allergic to gold
because his hair turned grey
after he started wearing a wedding band.

Work fascinates me –
I could sit and
look at it for hours.

My get up and go –
got up and went.

My poor performance in college
wasn't all my fault.
The kid that I cheated off of
never applied himself.

Are 21st birthdays important
because it marks the point
that kids start using their own IDs?

My fixed income is in serious disrepair.

I am buying more M&Ms
as I was advised to eat more greens.

My plans to quit drinking went awry.

I noticed an increase in graffiti in our area –
someone has been painting wheelchairs
in all the really good parking spaces.

I said to my doctor:

"Tell me straight,
do I have diabetes?
And don't sugar coat it."

Chapter 6

The Perplexing

Do the naughty children of environmentalists
get hydrogen fuel cells
in their Christmas stockings?

How does the city of Venice, Italy know
when there is a water main break?

Why do fast food restaurants
that offer free soft drink refills –
offer 3 sizes?

If the plural of mouse is mice,
why then isn't the plural
of blouse – blice?

If you go to see a psychic and
they require that you to make
an appointment – BEWARE!

If they truly were psychic,
wouldn't they already know
you were coming?

Why do we refer to it as
spare change?
Did anyone ever have a nickel,
dime or quarter get a flat?

Which is more expensive?

A road sign indicating a bump ahead

OR

fixing the bump?

Do people with multiple personalities
ask for separate checks
when dining alone?

Why did Kamikaze pilots
wear helmets?

Why are there signs in hotels, etc.
that indicate the fact that
seeing-eye dogs are permitted?

The only people that these signs pertain to
CANNOT SEE THE SIGNS!

Why are drive-up ATM machines
marked in braille?

What does one say to
an atheist who sneezes?

(Suggestion: "Serves you right.")

What does one say to
an agnostic who sneezes ?

(Suggestion: "Maybe you'll get better.")

Do cars with daytime running lights
automatically get
hot wax at the car wash?

Why do condemned criminals
get an alcohol swab
before receiving their lethal injection?

Modern day example of *existentialism*:

The person who spends hundreds of dollars
to tint their car windows
to then "flip off" a fellow driver who,
because of the window tint,
cannot see the insult.

Where is the *front of the church*?

If you meet in *front of the church*,
you would presumably meet
by the entrance doors.

Once you go through the doors,
you are now in the back of the church.

Now to go from the *front of the church*
to the *front of the church*
requires a long walk up the aisle.

If gun control advocates blame
gun manufacturers for gun crimes,
then why can't students blame
pen manufacturers for poor test grades?

If Shakespeare had written *The Godfather*:

"Leaveth thine dagger,
take thouest cannoli."

About the Author . . .

Peter D. Carlisi was born in 1948 and grew up in Yonkers, New York. He is the younger of two children with an older brother. He attended Catholic Schools through grade 12 after which he earned a Bachelor of Arts degree at Pace University in Pleasantville, New York having majored in History. Peter worked mainly in sales throughout his career most of which was in automotive replacement parts. In 1982 Peter moved to Long Island and was married to Mary (Chris) Gelmetti, a registered nurse who had earned a Bachelor of Science degree in nursing from Northeastern University in Boston, Massachusetts. They have two sons, Peter and Richard and relocated to the Saratoga Springs area of upstate New York to enjoy a more wholesome lifestyle and better educational opportunities for their children. Their older son, Peter graduated from Rensselaer Polytechnic Institute in Troy, New York and is a Captain in the US Air Force. Richard has a BA/MA in Music Education from Crane School of Music at SUNY Potsdam. He is planning to enter the US Military later this year. Peter D. is now retired, or as he likes to put it, "gainfully unemployed."